The Rules of the Game:
Inside the Corporate
Board Room

The Rules of the Game:
Inside the Corporate
Board Room

Thomas L. Whisler

DOW JONES-IRWIN
Homewood, Illinois 60430

© DOW JONES-IRWIN, 1984

ISBN 0-87094-463-0

Library of Congress Catalog Card No. 83-71841

Printed in the United States of America

1 2 3 4 5 6 7 8 9 0 K 1 0 9 8 7 6 5 4

PREFACE

This book presents the world of those who govern America's largest corporations, and presents it in the direct and personal terms of their values, their responsibilities, and their problems. These corporate directors, truly the elite of American business, work in very private fashion, behind the closed doors of the boardroom. Even though most of us are aware that the activities of very large corporations touch our lives in many ways, we have only a dim notion of what directors do, why they are there, and how they go about their business.

Two of us in the University of Chicago Graduate School of Business—Professor Paul M. Hirsch and I—were intrigued by this lack of information on director attitudes and behavior, and designed a research project aimed at learning more about them. An important part of the project was the interviewing of individual directors.

For more than three years, three of us—Professor Hirsch, my wife, Judith

Whisler, and I—traveled across the United States interviewing more than sixty directors, promising complete anonymity. Most served on the boards of *Fortune* 500 companies. We made an interesting discovery. Although these directors are relatively few in number, live in widely scattered areas and, for the most part, are strangers one to the other, they share common views, common values, common beliefs. They have their code, their culture—an unwritten set of rules that most of them voluntarily follow in governing the corporation.

In short, they have their Rules of the Game—presented in this book.

Thomas L. Whisler

TABLE OF

CONTENTS

ARTICLE I
INSIDE THE
BOARDROOM

Rule I (A)
NO FIGHTING

In reaching decisions on the use of corporate resources we face great uncertainty. Agreement and rational decisions are possible only through analysis and dialogue, not through aggression and threat. Respect for others' opinions, clarity in presenting one's own, and a sense of stewardship are the marks of a good director. A need to win is not. Don't forget that a boardroom fight can raise questions in the mind of investors about the quality of corporate governance and, hence, the future health of the company.

True Story

So strong among directors is the awareness of the negative impact of news on boardroom disharmony that, if impulsive outbursts or quarrels do occur, they are almost always contained and resolved quickly. One very strong-minded director (an entrepreneur in his own right) criticized the CEO openly at a board meeting. (See Rule I B.) Following the meeting the angry CEO suggested that the director resign, a suggestion promptly accepted. Very early the following morning the CEO telephoned the director, requesting that he not resign, acknowledging the merit of the director's criticism, and suggesting that it would not benefit the company were the resignation to occur. The director agreed, and stayed on the board. He remains there today. Both he and the CEO tread more carefully now.

Rule I (B)
SUPPORT YOUR
CEO

We, the board, chose the CEO (or we choose to keep the CEO). His success validates our wisdom; failure calls it into question. The job of CEO is a complex and demanding one; the pressures are enormous. In working with the CEO, we must distinguish between counsel and criticism. He will, or should, heed the former. Too much of the latter means that one of us should depart.

Rule I (C)
SERVE YOUR
APPRENTICESHIP

As a first-time director, you have a lot to learn—all of the Rules of the Game, in fact. If you have been on other boards, then you know that every board also tends to have its own practical rules for working together. In either case, (as first-timer or as old-timer) listen, watch, and learn after joining a board. Ask questions of your fellows—but in the cloakroom, not in the boardroom. Make your apprenticeship intensive but short. You have been invited onto the board with the expectation that you have a contribution to make. The board is waiting for it.

Rule I (D)
NO CRUSADES

The basic goals and purposes of a business corporation are surely known to all directors: We as directors seek not to reform society, but to serve its needs through honest and effective corporate performance by providing goods and services. The basic function of the board of directors is to assure that these corporate goals are achieved. Little enough time is available to get this job done, since a board meets only four to six times a year. The distraction imposed by a boardroom crusader can seriously affect board performance.

To the director with a mission: Do your crusading elsewhere; however, see Rule V E.

Rule I (E)
DO YOUR
HOMEWORK

You have been chosen to be a director because you have proven your competence, wisdom, and good judgment. But don't forget that today the fight for corporate survival and growth takes place in a world of rapid change involving new and knowledgeable competitors, new technologies, volatile political conditions. One wins through thoughtful planning and staying on top of current problems. Study the information given to you. Call for more if you want it. Directors are expected to be sharpshooters, not hipshooters.

Rule I (F)
PARTICIPATE

Directors play a unique role in the corporation. Some of the things that we are legally required to do are pedestrian (such as banking resolutions), but we must be prepared to make fateful and difficult decisions, decisions which require all of our collective experience and knowledge.

So, be present, be thoughtful, be participative. This is not a spectator sport.

ARTICLE II
UNDERSTANDING
WHY WE ARE HERE

Rule II (A)
WE ARE HERE TO GIVE
COUNSEL, MAKE JUDGMENTS,
AND OVERSEE THE
COMMITMENT OF
CORPORATE RESOURCES

While these responsibilities sound very broad and general, they become useful policy guides for our behavior as directors. We should, self-consciously, check what we are doing at any moment to see if our activity fits within these guidelines. If it doesn't, it means that, with few exceptions, we are doing something that is properly the province of management.

The province of management is the daily operation of the company, the direction of activities of others, the implementation of corporate strategy. Any exception to the Rule must be regarded as a crisis. An example of such a crisis would be the sudden and unexpected loss of the CEO and senior management through accident or resignation. Another

would be the demand of outsiders—
possibly the banks, possibly the court—
that the board remove management and
initiate an immediate change in corporate activities.

In any such crises, our overriding
objective is the early restoration of
effective management and our own re-
sumption of the role of governance—
which includes seeing to it that such
crises don't arise in the future.

Rule II (B)

WE ARE RESPONSIBLE FOR ASSESSING AND, IF NECESSARY, REPLACING TOP MANAGEMENT

This is uniquely our responsibility and authority. It is a responsibility only occasionally exercised, but we should never forget it.

Many of the Rules of the Game are directed toward establishing and maintaining the atmosphere of mutual respect and trust that must exist for us to function effectively with the CEO in the governance of the corporation. Properly established, we are a group of peers and not a court of review and inquiry, as some theorists would have us be, nor a group of rubber stamps, as some cynics would make us out to be. But, although we are peers, we must never forget that one of us—the CEO—stands in a special relationship to the rest. He or she may function as our chairman, but only through our acquiescence. We have made an implicit pledge to the rest of the world that the CEO will remain the chief only so long as he or she earns that right.

Rule II (C)
WE DON'T MANAGE
THE COMPANY

This is a Rule that the rest of the world finds difficult to understand. After all, the board is always shown at the top of the organization chart. But a moment's thought should convince anyone that a group of individuals who get together every month or two cannot be seriously regarded as managing the company. We govern; the executives manage. This distinction is obvious to directors who are themselves busy executives in other companies.

(*Note:* To directors from a nonbusiness background: Heed the Rules of the Game, and resist any temptation to dabble in management.)

Rule II (D)
WE DON'T SET
STRATEGY

This Rule is full of subtleties. To begin, if the board were to set strategy it would, in the process, lose the capacity and responsibility for objectively questioning and evaluating strategy alternatives. It would also be violating a precept that has slowly but surely become accepted as a management maxim: Those responsible for implementing strategy should play a major role in developing it; those who set strategy should be responsible for its implementation. Properly, then, those who set strategy (top management) explain it, defend it (and perhaps modify it) under the critical eye of a group of wise and experienced individuals (the board). Despite these caveats, the board bears the basic responsibility for insisting that the CEO develop a sound and explicit strategy for the company.

Rule II (E)
WE ARE RESPONSIBLE FOR
ASSURING LONG-RUN
SURVIVAL OF THE FIRM

We must always be mindful of the forces affecting the welfare of the company—social, political, and economic—and see to it that their implications are analyzed and evaluated by management and the board.

We are expected to have the broad, objective view of the true generalist. Managers come and go; the internal structure shifts and changes; there are acquisitions and divestitures. The board persists, dedicated to maintaining the viability of the corporation.

Rule II (F)
WE CANNOT
ABDICATE OUR
RESPONSIBILITIES

If we keep clearly in mind the difference between governance and management and understand why these two functions historically have been assigned to separate groups, we realize that it is impossible to delegate governance responsibilities to the executive staff.

If we understand this much, surely then we understand that abdicating these responsibilities could lead to disaster. The prospect of such a disaster leads some observers to propose adoption of a legal code of board responsibilities. In some companies an internal formal code is adopted. It is doubtful that either effort is better than the continual adherence among directors to the Rules of the Game and to the culture of which they are a part.

Perhaps our most critical responsibility is that of maintaining the quality of our board. We should not tolerate a poor director any more than we do a poor CEO. Either we police ourselves, or we will be policed.

Rule II (G)

OFFICIALLY, WE ARE HERE TO ACT IN THE SHAREHOLDERS' INTERESTS

This Rule is a rhetorical convenience that, unfortunately, has led to foolishness in lawsuits and, occasionally, to annoying shareholder behavior at the annual meeting. Shareholders can have all sorts of diverse and conflicting individual interests. Fortunately, an exchange exists where conflicts and change can be resolved through buying and selling of shares.

Strictly speaking then, we don't seek to serve these interests directly. We do, however, watch shareholder sentiment in the market, for it tells us how well we are doing. The behavior of the price of our shares is a measure of the collective judgment of investors about the long-run prospects of our company. A more accurate statement would be that we act to maximize the economic value of the firm. This is a hard one to explain to the rest of the world. So, we are stuck with an "official" Rule . . . but we should keep our own thinking straight.

ARTICLE III
OUTSIDE THE
BOARDROOM

Rule III (A)
KEEP YOUR DISTANCE FROM
SUBORDINATE COMPANY
EXECUTIVES

Most boards have as directors some senior executives employed by the firm. These inside directors are privy to the same information as outsiders, and have the same status. (Except that they often get no directors' fees and may be barred from certain board committees, such as audit and compensation.)

As directors they are *peers* inside the boardroom. Outside the boardroom they are something less, so distance must be kept from them as from other second- and third-line executives. The reason for maintaining distance? Scrupulous avoidance of even the appearance of going around the chief executive.

True Story

One outside director said, "If I were contacted by an inside director, alleging some malfeasance, I would listen. But, he had better be absolutely correct in his charges." (See Rule VII B.)

Rule III (B)
BE PREPARED TO COUNSEL,
INDIVIDUALLY, WITH
THE CEO

Other Rules (VI B, II A) point up the counseling relationship of the board, as a whole, with the CEO. This kind of counseling usually takes place within the boardroom or at dinner the night before the meeting. Outside the boardroom, counseling may continue, most often as a one-on-one relationship. You may be especially qualified to help with a specific problem. The telephone is the usual medium, although the CEO or you may use a business trip as an opportunity for dinner and discussion.

Occasionally, the counseling relationship may become more general in nature with the discovery that there is "good chemistry" between you and the chief executive. You become, in effect, an especially trusted counselor and friend, in addition to being one of the members of the board.

Caveat

Such a relationship is acceptable and helpful, but don't allow it to put you at odds with your fellow directors. There is no place for a Rasputin on a board.

Rule III (C)
DON'T DISCUSS
COMPANY BUSINESS
WITH OTHERS

This Rule seems too obvious to require elaboration. But leaks of critical information do occur and, occasionally, a foolish director is at fault. If you value your reputation as a director (and this reputation has value in the marketplace), don't discuss anything that isn't already in the public domain. A close-mouthed director is a good director.

Rule III (D)
WATCH FOR
STRAWS IN
THE WIND

As a director you are never off duty. The company, its needs, its vulnerabilities, and its plans for the future should be in your head wherever you go. That way, any information that you acquire, or events that you witness, can be automatically assessed for relevance to the welfare of the company. This information might be related to new economic developments, to new management techniques, or to new concepts and ideas gleaned from seminars and conferences. Use the telephone and pass information on to the CEO for exploration, or to fellow directors for evaluation. The close-mouthed director should keep ears and eyes open.

Rule III (E)
WATCH FOR
TALENT

The director with business experience knows that a talented individual is one of the most valuable resources the firm can acquire. When you encounter an outstanding individual outside the company your directorial instincts should lead you to bring that person to the attention of management. When you encounter such a person inside the company you should discuss with your fellow directors and the CEO the desirability of marking him or her for succession to the top.

ARTICLE IV

ASSESSING BOARD

INVITATIONS

Rule IV (A)
JOIN A WINNER. YOU ARE WHAT YOUR BOARD (AND ITS COMPANY) IS

In the world of business and corporate affairs your reputation as a director is strongly affected by the quality of the boards on which you sit. So your choice of boards, if you have a choice, is not a trivial one. In fact, no board at all is better than a bad one. Some guidelines:

- Avoid poor economic performers. Always study the corporate financials, the share price history, before you sign on. Seek the opinion of a competent security analyst and of other knowledgeable individuals. Why book a berth on the Titanic after the iceberg?
- Avoid noisy boards full of conflict. Such boards are the journalists' delight. But you do your professional reputation little good by being

recorded as being present at a board-room fight. (See Rule I A.)

- Big, rich, and prestigious companies are the most desirable. The general assumption is that such organizations know what they are doing, including inviting you to join.

Whatever your choice, never forget to clear your decision to join a new board with the board of your own company before making it final. Also, you never forget that while your personal attributes are very important, your value in the market (for directors) derives, to a great extent, from the executive positions that you hold. (See Rule V A.)

Rule IV (B)
TRY TO STAY
CLOSE TO HOME

The great enemy is travel time. It can add as much as three quarters of the total time that is devoted to a board meeting. True, the time spent on the airplane going to the meeting can be used to study materials related to the subjects to be discussed. But "dead heading" home can seem like valuable time forever lost.

An invitation to join a board that meets just across town or that requires only a two-hour drive is appealing. But there can be costs. A convenient board may be an uninteresting one, the company second-rate. Too many convenient boards make you a "local," out of it on the national scene. You may find yourself sitting down over and over with the same crowd in different boardrooms. The opportunities for learning are thus constrained. The "movable feast" of the same local directors sitting together in different boardrooms can also raise questions of conflict of interest, of groupthink, and of insularity.

If you are in a large metropolitan area, you can invoke the close-to-home rule rather often. But no matter where you are, if one of the top corporations calls you, it is close enough.

Rule IV (C)
DECLINE OR RESIGN
OFFICIALLY ONLY FOR
REASONS OF OVERLOAD

This Rule implies that an "unofficial" reason may exist. Putting aside the case where the invited executive is beyond doubt very pressed for time, the situation can easily arise in which an invitation is extended to join a board that has no appeal. Basic good manners requires that a turndown should have as little hurt in it as possible, and that the excuse for refusal have high credibility. After all, the invitation generally has been carefully thought out by the board that invites you. Since it is a general belief among executives that there is never enough time, overload is a universally acceptable reason for declining.

Resigning a board is another matter; more than good manners is involved. It is important that a resignation not raise a question in the marketplace about the state of corporate affairs. The *proper* way is to serve out your term and indicate, with regret, that you cannot stand for reelection for reasons of overload. But, if you make this move, don't immediately join another board or you may raise questions about your personal credibility, and (in the market) about the state of affairs in the board you left.

Rule IV (D)
TRADE UP
SLOWLY AND
UNOBTRUSIVELY

Some directors will find this Rule puzzling. But directors of outstanding reputation, who usually have open invitations to join other boards, will understand. The incentive to "trade up" is strong. Membership on the board of a large and prominent company promises new experiences and insights, new associates. The caveats stated in this Rule—"slowly" and "unobtrusively"—reflect the conflict between the need of the corporation, for a stable and committed set of directors, and the need of the individual to continue an upward career movement. Moving too often and too obviously will be self-defeating. Other directors will begin to doubt your real interest in contributing to the effective governance of any corporation.

Rule IV (E)

OFFICIALLY, DEPRECATE THE PERSONAL SIGNIFICANCE OF YOUR DIRECTOR'S FEE

You are *invited* onto a board; you are not hired. You are a wise and watchful counselor, not an employee. You are an eminent person. No company will offer a director's fee that, in itself, is adequate compensation for your time. Prestige and admission to the elite make up the difference. On the other hand, five or six directorships can produce a gratifying income. Nevertheless, obey this Rule.

True Story

One eminent public figure, tentatively offered a directorship on a major corporate board, responded by asking how much it paid. The offer was withdrawn. Never ask. You can always look up the fee in published documents.

ARTICLE V
GETTING NEW
BLOOD

Rule V (A)
PRIME BEEF = CEOs OF OTHER COMPANIES (BIG AND RICH IS BEST)

We want winners—winners in the Game in which we play. If we were to examine a portrait of the *ideal* corporate board, we would note immediately the presence of a large number of chief executive officers from other companies. The reason for this dominant group is not mysterious. The objective is to bring into the boardroom the kind of wisdom that is gained by being responsible for the fate of a corporation. Note, however, that the ideal is not to have the board made up *exclusively* of chief executive officers. Certain other perspectives are valuable also. But, if a choice is forced the nod must go to a CEO, and (again ideally) one from a large and successful company.

The importance of being a CEO is very clear to those who have achieved this status.

True Story

One executive recalls, "I remember that before my appointment (as CEO) was announced, I had been invited only onto our own board. Within a few months after the announcement I had fifteen or twenty overtures to join onto other boards. It seems hard to believe. I was still the same person. Before, I seemed to be nobody; afterward, I was wanted by everyone."

Rule V (B)
TRY TO ADD
LUSTER TO
THE BOARD

This Rule differs from the preceding one, even though the difference may not be immediately obvious. While the argument for bringing the business wisdom of a CEO into the boardroom is persuasive, there are additional considerations. Adding luster is one. What is meant by "luster" is the quality of the individual director's reputation—a quality that usually comes from recognized achievement in an important field. Achievement in business, yes; but also achievement in science, in political affairs, in military and professional activities, in academic leadership. We seek to do this because we believe that it enhances the credibility of the board in the eyes of key outsiders and, most important, makes it easier to attract the best candidates when we seek new board members. Call it a "bandwagon effect" if you like, but don't discount its importance.

Rule V (C)
WE SHOULD SEEK TO ADD A WOMAN OR A MINORITY GROUP MEMBER TO THE BOARD, BUT ONLY IF THEY ARE "TRULY QUALIFIED"

Of all the Rules, this is the lengthiest; and of all the Rules, this is the most controversial, no matter how it is stated. The word *should* implies an intention to change an established way of doing things; but it is an intention that, in many cases, hasn't yet been carried out. The last phrase in the Rule has a tendency to become a justification or reason for not having taken action. When social and political pressures are being felt in the boardroom, there should be recognition of the importance of adapting to them in ways consistent with keeping the corporation strong.

But this adaptation seems to come into conflict with other Rules, like those barring crusades and crusaders (in this case, a crusade to add new kinds of members), and the Rule placing overwhelming priority on seeking chief executive officers as new board members. The number of women and minority group members who are corporate CEOs is small, and it is obvious that to take the action implied in this Rule we will have to look at other kinds of positions and occupations. In the last analysis, the response to this Rule is likely to depend upon the position taken by the chairman of our board. His position, in turn, will probably reflect the board's collective degree of comfort in letting things remain just as they are.

Rule V (D)
LOOK HARD AT LAWYERS,
INVESTMENT BANKERS, AND
CONSULTANTS BEFORE
INVITING THEM ONTO
THE BOARD

This Rule seems quite vague and almost too broad in scope. After all, what do these three occupations have in common that should cause one to look at their members with a cold eye? It may be the fact that their living is made by selling advice, developed in part from their access to information—sometimes very sensitive information—that results from their relationships with various corporations.

If the relationship is kept at the consultant-client level, control can be maintained over access to information. But in the boardroom, ideally, nothing important is held back. Investment bankers, in particular, can be worrisome, because of the fear that they or their colleagues might engineer an unfriendly takeover, based upon privileged information.

There is need to remember the other side of the coin, however. The very breadth of exposure of the individuals in these professions can give them a unique and valuable perspective, one that no CEO is likely to have. These individuals, as directors, often play a significant counseling role to the chief executive.

So it's a question of uncertain loyalties versus broad insight and perspective on the world. We should take an initial hard look, yes, but be willing to bring in those we trust. As is so often the case in corporate life, the key word is *trust*.

Rule V (E)
NO CRUSADERS

This Rule, a counterpart of Rule I D banning crusades in the boardroom, may seem repetitious. It's not, because it serves an important function as a guideline in assessing potential board candidates, whereas the earlier Rule simply expressed the code governing activity in the boardroom. As a guideline, it may get in the way of our efforts to implement the Rules in this chapter relating to adding luster to the board, to adding a woman or minority person, or even to bringing in a CEO.

It's not that we want a board made up of dummies or Milquetoasts. It's just that we don't want someone whose devotion is more to a cause or to a constituency than to the well-being of the corporation.

It's not always easy to implement this Rule. We may encounter the "closet crusader" whose tendencies are not apparent before coming on the board.

True Story

A scientist, invited onto the board of a company that published school texts in the sciences, became openly critical of what he saw as his fellow-directors' single-minded interest in the bottom line—the market appeal and profitability of the texts—in contrast to his own concern over improving their quality. When his term expired he was not renominated. He was perceived as a crusader.

ARTICLE VI
ASSESSING
THE CEO

Rule VI (A)

HE SHOULD HAVE A PLAN
FOR MAKING THE COMPANY
BIGGER AND RICHER

Perhaps a more elegant (and technically accurate) phrasing of this Rule is that the CEO should have a strategy for enhancing the economic value of the company. In the marketplace, where share prices reflect expectations about the company's future, the growth in assets, sales, market share, and earnings become measures of enhanced economic value now and in the future.

This Rule begs only one question: Bigger and richer, *when?* We, as directors, who are responsible for the long-run well-being of the company, must answer this question. We must take responsibility, also, for deciding how risky a strategy we will follow.

But we expect the CEO to provide a well-thought-out plan with any necessary choices clearly marked and well researched. If the CEO doesn't do this, the company and the board (if it goes along) drift without direction. There is no more critical measure of a CEO than developing and implementing an effective corporate strategy.

Rule VI (B)
HE SHOULD HEED
OUR COUNSEL

To "heed" means "to pay attention to." When the CEO solicits our counsel it is reasonable to believe that he pays attention to it. It doesn't necessarily mean that he must follow it. If we volunteer our counsel, it is reasonable to expect him to listen, to respond with his assessment of it. Again, it doesn't mean that he must follow it. If he neither solicits our counsel nor listens to it, he signals that he believes he doesn't need us. In that event, the Rules of the Game are being violated. Then, either we, as individuals, choose to resign, or we, as a board, begin to assert a stronger role in governance by investing more effort in assessment and audit of corporate performance or by demanding more information about operations. Apparent successful corporate performance doesn't absolve us from responsibility for action—the potential for disaster may lurk behind the facade of success. If our best efforts at communicating meet a stonewall, we may want to consider a change of CEO.

True Story

Despite the doubts of a number of his directors, a strong-minded CEO received permission to build a new manufacturing facility. Soon after this plant went into operation, it became clear that it was unprofitable. The board advised the CEO that he should either develop a specific plan for making it profitable or else shut it down and sell it. Although the losses continued, the CEO developed no plan. The board recommended shutdown of the plant. The CEO, sure of a turnaround in profitability ignored the recommendation. The board then advised the CEO that his employment was terminated. His successor shut the plant and sold it.

Rule VI (C)
HE SHOULD HAVE
OUTSTANDING
SUBORDINATES

Our basic responsibility for assuring the long-run survival and economic well-being of the firm is carried out not by our managing the firm but by our seeing to it that competent managers are in place and doing their jobs well.

We give the CEO freedom to build a management team, but we must assure that he chooses first-rate executives. Therefore, we ask that these executives appear before us occasionally and describe their activities so we may assess them. The selection of the chief executive is a difficult and risky decision, one that a board faces only infrequently. This decision is made far easier and less uncertain if potential candidates have been observed at close hand over a period of time. Thus, the competence and quality of the CEO is reasonably judged by the quality of the subordinates he chooses.

Rule VI (D)
HE SHOULD NOT
SURPRISE US

We can give deliberate care and thought to the important corporate issues only if they are laid out in advance of discussion and decision. The unpleasant surprise of finding a mass of new and unfamiliar material waiting on the boardroom table when we sit down at the meeting is matched only by learning in the meeting that an action item that wasn't listed in the agenda must be handled. Worst of all is learning for the first time of some difficulty in our corporation by reading about it in the newspaper. All of these surprises represent an inadequate communication effort on the part of the CEO. Too many surprises might, one day, call forth a big one from us.

Rule VI (E)
HE SHOULD TELL
US ALL

At least, all that we need to know when major action is to be taken, when events significant to the corporation are occurring, when trouble is brewing. And our questions are to be treated seriously. Concealment leads to suspicion, oversight to frustration, indifference to resentment.

More than feelings are involved.

True Story

One director, accustomed to complete openness on the part of the CEO suddenly found himself on a new board that resulted from his company's being acquired. There he found the new CEO playing a game of minimal disclosure. This director and another (also new) were stonewalled when they asked for more information. Electing not to resign, he later found himself (along with the rest of the board) the target of legal suits after the company failed. He was sued on the grounds that he had knowingly withheld information from the shareholders!

ARTICLE VII
FLUSHING
THE CEO

Rule VII (A)
DON'T RUSH

Removing the chief executive officer is a last resort. It may signal one or more of many things to the world outside— that a conflict of judgment has developed at the governance level, that the conflict could not be reconciled through compromise, that the CEO could not run the firm successfully, that the board is seeking to intervene in the management of the company, or that the board has an "adversary" concept of its role.

Perhaps none of these are true, and perhaps the action is in the best interests of the company; but just as divorce seems to many to signify a failure to resolve marital problems in the most effective way, flushing the CEO seems to signify less than optimal functioning of the governance process. A new CEO will now be required, of course.

The best potential outside candidates for the job may be wary of the situation into which they would be moving. (How long will the next CEO last?) The best senior managers in the company, unless offered the top position, may well decide that it is time to look elsewhere before the new chief arrives. As a director, you can expect to devote more time than you wish to deliberating with your colleagues about taking such disruptive action. If you do it, you will certainly be motivated to do everything you can to avoid having to do it again.

Rule VII (B)
MAKE SURE OF
OVERWHELMING
DIRECTOR SUPPORT

Ousting of the CEO reflects a judgment—that, of all the factors contributing to unsatisfactory corporate performance, inadequate management is clearly preeminent. This judgment must be so widely shared by the board that any overt action results in the CEO's departure. An abortive attempt at ouster calls into question the competence of the board to govern and signals the existence of a fight. (See Rule I A.)

Finally, remember that inside directors are in a most uncomfortable spot. While they may provide valuable information, they may not wish to be party to overt actions in a palace coup. This is largely the outside director's Game. (Did anyone say that being a director is easy?)

Rule VII (C)
DON'T WAIT
TOO LONG

The thoughtful and timely resolution of issues, where high uncertainty and substantial differences of perspective exist, requires respect for the judgment of your colleagues (including the CEO) as well as a willingness to seek consensus. However, preservation of harmony should not become an end in itself.

If the CEO persists against all advice in taking managerial actions that the directors know to be inappropriate, or does not deal effectively with inadequate corporate performance, then immediate removal is desirable.

Investor confidence in a company with a dilatory board evaporates. Competent director candidates are reluctant to join such a board. Good executives within the company will become aware of a problem and look for greener fields. If you are beginning to feel uneasy about the

CEO's performance, you must, at the very least, ask other outside directors if they share your uneasiness.

True Story

The board of one large company, moving in deliberate fashion, required a year and a half to complete the flush. That was too long. The market had already decided that the board was incompetent as well as the management. Takeover loomed.